50 Premium Beef Dinner Recipes

By: Kelly Johnson

Table of Contents

- Filet Mignon with Garlic Butter
- Beef Wellington
- Prime Rib Roast
- Braised Short Ribs
- Beef Bourguignon
- Ribeye Steak with Chimichurri
- Porterhouse Steak with Herb Butter
- T-Bone Steak with Red Wine Sauce
- Grilled Flank Steak with Chimichurri
- Beef Stroganoff
- Slow-Cooked Brisket
- New York Strip Steak with Peppercorn Sauce
- Beef Tenderloin with Blue Cheese Sauce
- Korean BBQ Beef (Bulgogi)
- Classic Beef Meatloaf
- Beef and Broccoli Stir-Fry
- Mongolian Beef
- Teriyaki Beef Skewers
- Spicy Thai Beef Salad
- Beef Enchiladas
- Beef Tacos with Pico de Gallo
- Beef Lasagna
- Beef Shepherd's Pie
- Italian Beef Braciole
- Beef Pot Pie
- Beef Kebab with Tzatziki Sauce
- Beef Quesadillas
- Beef and Mushroom Stroganoff
- Slow-Cooked Beef Chili
- Beef and Guinness Stew
- Beef Sliders with Caramelized Onions
- Beef Ragu with Pappardelle
- Beef Goulash
- Balsamic Glazed Beef Medallions
- Pho Bo (Vietnamese Beef Noodle Soup)

- Beef Carpaccio
- Grilled Beef Satay with Peanut Sauce
- Beef Empanadas
- Beef Picadillo
- Beef Rouladen (German Stuffed Beef Rolls)
- Beef Sushi Rolls
- Beef Pho with Fresh Herbs
- Slow-Cooked Beef Barbacoa
- Beef Tostadas with Avocado Salsa
- Beef Korma
- Beef and Eggplant Stir-Fry
- Beef Kebab with Moroccan Spices
- Beef Fajitas with Bell Peppers
- Steak Diane
- Beef Tamales

Filet Mignon with Garlic Butter

Ingredients:

- 4 filet mignon steaks
- 4 tbsp unsalted butter
- 2 cloves garlic, minced
- 1 tsp fresh thyme leaves
- Salt and pepper to taste

Instructions:

1. Preheat oven to 400°F (200°C).
2. Season steaks with salt and pepper.
3. In a skillet over medium-high heat, sear steaks for 2-3 minutes per side.
4. Transfer skillet to the oven and roast for 6-8 minutes for medium-rare.
5. Meanwhile, melt butter in a small saucepan, add garlic and thyme, and cook until fragrant.
6. Drizzle garlic butter over steaks before serving.

Beef Wellington

Ingredients:

- 1.5 lbs beef tenderloin
- 2 tbsp olive oil
- 2 tbsp Dijon mustard
- 1 sheet puff pastry
- 4 oz prosciutto
- 1 egg, beaten
- Salt and pepper to taste

Instructions:

1. Preheat oven to 425°F (220°C).
2. Sear the beef tenderloin in olive oil until browned on all sides. Let cool.
3. Brush beef with Dijon mustard.
4. Lay prosciutto on puff pastry, place beef on top, and roll to encase.
5. Brush with beaten egg and bake for 20-25 minutes or until pastry is golden.
6. Let rest for 10 minutes before slicing.

Prime Rib Roast

Ingredients:

- 1 prime rib roast (5-6 lbs)
- 2 tbsp olive oil
- 4 cloves garlic, minced
- 2 tbsp fresh rosemary, chopped
- Salt and pepper to taste

Instructions:

1. Preheat oven to 450°F (230°C).
2. Rub roast with olive oil, garlic, rosemary, salt, and pepper.
3. Place roast in a roasting pan and cook for 30 minutes.
4. Reduce heat to 325°F (165°C) and continue cooking for 1.5-2 hours for medium-rare.
5. Let rest for 20 minutes before carving.

Braised Short Ribs

Ingredients:

- 4 lbs beef short ribs
- 2 tbsp olive oil
- 1 onion, chopped
- 3 cloves garlic, minced
- 2 cups beef broth
- 1 cup red wine
- 2 tbsp tomato paste
- Salt and pepper to taste

Instructions:

1. Preheat oven to 325°F (165°C).
2. Season short ribs with salt and pepper and brown in olive oil.
3. Remove ribs, sauté onion and garlic, then add tomato paste.
4. Deglaze with red wine and beef broth.
5. Return ribs to the pot, cover, and braise in the oven for 2.5-3 hours.

Beef Bourguignon

Ingredients:

- 2 lbs beef chuck, cut into cubes
- 4 strips bacon, chopped
- 1 onion, chopped
- 2 carrots, sliced
- 2 cloves garlic, minced
- 2 cups red wine
- 1 cup beef broth
- 2 tbsp tomato paste
- 1 bay leaf
- Salt and pepper to taste

Instructions:

1. Preheat oven to 350°F (175°C).
2. Brown bacon in a Dutch oven, remove and set aside.
3. Brown beef in the bacon fat, remove and set aside.
4. Sauté onion, carrots, and garlic, then stir in tomato paste.
5. Add wine, broth, bay leaf, and beef. Cover and bake for 2.5-3 hours.

Ribeye Steak with Chimichurri

Ingredients:

- 2 ribeye steaks
- 2 tbsp olive oil
- 1 cup fresh parsley, chopped
- 3 cloves garlic, minced
- 1/4 cup red wine vinegar
- 1/2 tsp red pepper flakes
- Salt and pepper to taste

Instructions:

1. Season steaks with salt and pepper.
2. Grill steaks over medium-high heat for 4-5 minutes per side for medium-rare.
3. In a bowl, mix parsley, garlic, red wine vinegar, olive oil, red pepper flakes, salt, and pepper.
4. Serve steaks with chimichurri sauce on top.

Porterhouse Steak with Herb Butter

Ingredients:

- 1 porterhouse steak
- 2 tbsp olive oil
- 4 tbsp unsalted butter, softened
- 1 tsp fresh thyme, chopped
- 1 tsp fresh rosemary, chopped
- Salt and pepper to taste

Instructions:

1. Preheat grill to high.
2. Season steak with olive oil, salt, and pepper.
3. Grill steak for 6-8 minutes per side for medium-rare.
4. Mix butter with thyme and rosemary.
5. Serve steak with a dollop of herb butter on top.

T-Bone Steak with Red Wine Sauce

Ingredients:

- 2 T-bone steaks
- 2 tbsp olive oil
- 1 cup red wine
- 1 shallot, minced
- 2 tbsp unsalted butter
- Salt and pepper to taste

Instructions:

1. Season steaks with salt and pepper.
2. Grill steaks over medium-high heat for 4-5 minutes per side for medium-rare.
3. In a pan, sauté shallot in olive oil, deglaze with red wine, and reduce by half.
4. Whisk in butter and season with salt and pepper.
5. Serve steaks with red wine sauce.

Grilled Flank Steak with Chimichurri

Ingredients:

- 1 flank steak
- 2 tbsp olive oil
- 1 cup fresh parsley, chopped
- 3 cloves garlic, minced
- 1/4 cup red wine vinegar
- 1/2 tsp red pepper flakes
- Salt and pepper to taste

Instructions:

1. Season steak with salt, pepper, and olive oil.
2. Grill over high heat for 4-5 minutes per side for medium-rare.
3. Mix parsley, garlic, red wine vinegar, olive oil, red pepper flakes, salt, and pepper.
4. Serve steak sliced thin with chimichurri sauce.

Beef Stroganoff

Ingredients:

- 1 lb beef sirloin, thinly sliced
- 2 tbsp olive oil
- 1 onion, chopped
- 2 cloves garlic, minced
- 8 oz mushrooms, sliced
- 1 cup beef broth
- 1 cup sour cream
- 1 tbsp Dijon mustard
- Salt and pepper to taste
- Cooked egg noodles or rice for serving

Instructions:

1. Heat olive oil in a skillet and brown beef slices, then set aside.
2. In the same skillet, sauté onion, garlic, and mushrooms until soft.
3. Add beef broth, bring to a simmer, and stir in sour cream and mustard.
4. Return beef to the skillet, season with salt and pepper, and cook for 5-7 minutes.
5. Serve over egg noodles or rice.

Slow-Cooked Brisket

Ingredients:

- 4 lbs beef brisket
- 2 tbsp olive oil
- 1 onion, sliced
- 3 cloves garlic, minced
- 1 cup beef broth
- 1/2 cup red wine
- 2 tbsp tomato paste
- 1 bay leaf
- Salt and pepper to taste

Instructions:

1. Season brisket with salt and pepper.
2. Brown brisket in olive oil in a large skillet.
3. Transfer to a slow cooker, add onion, garlic, beef broth, wine, tomato paste, and bay leaf.
4. Cook on low for 8 hours or until tender.
5. Slice and serve with the cooking juices.

New York Strip Steak with Peppercorn Sauce

Ingredients:

- 2 New York strip steaks
- 2 tbsp olive oil
- 1/4 cup brandy or cognac
- 1/2 cup heavy cream
- 2 tbsp green peppercorns, crushed
- Salt and pepper to taste

Instructions:

1. Season steaks with salt and pepper.
2. Heat olive oil in a skillet and cook steaks to desired doneness, then set aside.
3. Deglaze the pan with brandy, then add heavy cream and green peppercorns.
4. Simmer until sauce thickens. Serve steaks with peppercorn sauce.

Beef Tenderloin with Blue Cheese Sauce

Ingredients:

- 2 beef tenderloin steaks
- 2 tbsp olive oil
- 1/2 cup heavy cream
- 1/4 cup crumbled blue cheese
- 1 tsp fresh thyme leaves
- Salt and pepper to taste

Instructions:

1. Preheat oven to 400°F (200°C).
2. Sear steaks in olive oil for 2-3 minutes per side, then roast in the oven for 6-8 minutes.
3. In a small saucepan, heat heavy cream and stir in blue cheese and thyme until smooth.
4. Season with salt and pepper and serve over steaks.

Korean BBQ Beef (Bulgogi)

Ingredients:

- 1 lb beef ribeye, thinly sliced
- 1/4 cup soy sauce
- 2 tbsp sesame oil
- 2 tbsp brown sugar
- 2 cloves garlic, minced
- 1 tsp grated ginger
- 1 tbsp sesame seeds
- 2 green onions, sliced

Instructions:

1. Mix soy sauce, sesame oil, brown sugar, garlic, ginger, and sesame seeds.
2. Marinate beef in the mixture for at least 30 minutes.
3. Grill or pan-fry beef over high heat until cooked through.
4. Garnish with green onions and serve with rice.

Classic Beef Meatloaf

Ingredients:

- 1 lb ground beef
- 1/2 cup breadcrumbs
- 1 egg, beaten
- 1/2 cup onion, chopped
- 2 cloves garlic, minced
- 1/4 cup ketchup
- 1 tbsp Worcestershire sauce
- Salt and pepper to taste

Instructions:

1. Preheat oven to 350°F (175°C).
2. In a bowl, mix ground beef, breadcrumbs, egg, onion, garlic, ketchup, Worcestershire sauce, salt, and pepper.
3. Shape into a loaf and place in a baking dish.
4. Bake for 1 hour. Let rest for 10 minutes before slicing.

Beef and Broccoli Stir-Fry

Ingredients:

- 1 lb beef flank steak, thinly sliced
- 2 cups broccoli florets
- 2 tbsp soy sauce
- 1 tbsp oyster sauce
- 1 tsp cornstarch
- 2 cloves garlic, minced
- 2 tbsp vegetable oil

Instructions:

1. Marinate beef in soy sauce, oyster sauce, and cornstarch for 15 minutes.
2. Heat oil in a wok and stir-fry garlic and beef until browned.
3. Add broccoli and stir-fry until tender-crisp.
4. Serve with rice or noodles.

Mongolian Beef

Ingredients:

- 1 lb beef sirloin, thinly sliced
- 1/4 cup soy sauce
- 2 tbsp brown sugar
- 1 tbsp hoisin sauce
- 2 cloves garlic, minced
- 1/2 tsp ginger, grated
- 2 tbsp vegetable oil
- Green onions, sliced

Instructions:

1. Combine soy sauce, brown sugar, hoisin sauce, garlic, and ginger.
2. Heat oil in a wok and stir-fry beef until browned.
3. Pour sauce over beef and cook until thickened.
4. Garnish with green onions and serve with rice.

Teriyaki Beef Skewers

Ingredients:

- 1 lb beef sirloin, cut into cubes
- 1/2 cup soy sauce
- 1/4 cup brown sugar
- 2 tbsp sesame oil
- 2 cloves garlic, minced
- 1 tsp grated ginger
- Wooden skewers, soaked

Instructions:

1. Mix soy sauce, brown sugar, sesame oil, garlic, and ginger in a bowl.
2. Marinate beef cubes in the mixture for at least 30 minutes.
3. Thread beef onto skewers.
4. Grill skewers over medium heat until beef is cooked through.

Spicy Thai Beef Salad

Ingredients:

- 1 lb beef sirloin, thinly sliced
- 1 tbsp vegetable oil
- 2 cups mixed greens
- 1 cucumber, sliced
- 1/4 cup red onion, thinly sliced
- 1/4 cup fresh cilantro
- 2 tbsp fish sauce
- 1 tbsp lime juice
- 1 tbsp chili paste
- 1 tsp sugar

Instructions:

1. Heat oil in a skillet and cook beef until browned. Set aside.
2. In a bowl, whisk fish sauce, lime juice, chili paste, and sugar.
3. Toss mixed greens, cucumber, onion, and cilantro with the dressing.
4. Top with beef slices and serve.

Beef Enchiladas

Ingredients:

- 1 lb ground beef
- 1 onion, chopped
- 1 cup enchilada sauce
- 8 flour tortillas
- 1 cup shredded cheddar cheese
- 1/4 cup sliced black olives (optional)

Instructions:

1. Preheat oven to 350°F (175°C).
2. Brown beef with onion, then mix in 1/2 cup enchilada sauce.
3. Fill tortillas with beef mixture, roll up, and place in a baking dish.
4. Top with remaining sauce, cheese, and olives.
5. Bake for 20 minutes or until cheese is melted.

Beef Tacos with Pico de Gallo

Ingredients:

- 1 lb ground beef
- 1 tbsp taco seasoning
- 8 taco shells
- 1 cup shredded lettuce
- 1/2 cup shredded cheese
- 1/2 cup sour cream
- Pico de Gallo (chopped tomatoes, onions, cilantro, lime juice, and salt)

Instructions:

1. Cook ground beef with taco seasoning.
2. Fill taco shells with beef, lettuce, cheese, sour cream, and Pico de Gallo.

Beef Lasagna

Ingredients:

- 1 lb ground beef
- 1 onion, chopped
- 3 cups marinara sauce
- 1 lb lasagna noodles
- 2 cups ricotta cheese
- 2 cups shredded mozzarella
- 1/2 cup grated Parmesan

Instructions:

1. Preheat oven to 375°F (190°C).
2. Cook ground beef with onion, then mix with marinara sauce.
3. Layer cooked noodles, beef sauce, ricotta, and mozzarella in a baking dish.
4. Repeat layers and top with Parmesan.
5. Bake for 30-40 minutes until bubbly.

Beef Shepherd's Pie

Ingredients:

- 1 lb ground beef
- 1 onion, chopped
- 2 cups mixed vegetables (peas, carrots, corn)
- 1 cup beef broth
- 4 cups mashed potatoes

Instructions:

1. Preheat oven to 400°F (200°C).
2. Brown beef with onion, then mix in vegetables and broth.
3. Spread beef mixture in a baking dish and top with mashed potatoes.
4. Bake for 25 minutes or until golden brown.

Italian Beef Braciole

Ingredients:

- 1 lb thinly sliced beef flank steak
- 1/4 cup breadcrumbs
- 1/4 cup grated Parmesan
- 2 tbsp chopped parsley
- 2 cloves garlic, minced
- 2 cups marinara sauce

Instructions:

1. Mix breadcrumbs, Parmesan, parsley, and garlic.
2. Spread mixture on beef slices, roll up, and secure with toothpicks.
3. Brown rolls in a skillet, then simmer in marinara sauce for 30 minutes.

Beef Pot Pie

Ingredients:

- 1 lb beef stew meat, cubed
- 1 onion, chopped
- 2 cups mixed vegetables (carrots, peas, potatoes)
- 1 cup beef broth
- 1 sheet puff pastry
- 1 egg, beaten

Instructions:

1. Preheat oven to 375°F (190°C).
2. Brown beef with onion, then mix in vegetables and broth.
3. Transfer to a baking dish, cover with puff pastry, and brush with egg.
4. Bake for 25-30 minutes until golden brown.

Beef Kebab with Tzatziki Sauce

Ingredients:

- 1 lb beef sirloin, cubed
- 1 tbsp olive oil
- 1 tsp dried oregano
- Salt and pepper to taste
- 1 cup Greek yogurt
- 1 cucumber, grated
- 1 clove garlic, minced
- 1 tbsp lemon juice
- Wooden skewers, soaked

Instructions:

1. Marinate beef in olive oil, oregano, salt, and pepper.
2. Thread beef onto skewers and grill until cooked to desired doneness.
3. Mix yogurt, cucumber, garlic, and lemon juice for tzatziki sauce.
4. Serve kebabs with tzatziki sauce.

Beef Quesadillas

Ingredients:

- 1 lb ground beef
- 1 tbsp taco seasoning
- 2 cups shredded cheese (cheddar or Mexican blend)
- 8 flour tortillas
- 1/4 cup chopped green onions
- Sour cream and salsa for serving

Instructions:

1. Cook ground beef with taco seasoning.
2. Heat a tortilla in a skillet, sprinkle with cheese, beef, and green onions.
3. Top with another tortilla, cook until cheese melts, then flip.
4. Cut into wedges and serve with sour cream and salsa.

Beef and Mushroom Stroganoff

Ingredients:

- 1 lb beef sirloin, sliced
- 2 cups mushrooms, sliced
- 1 onion, chopped
- 1 cup beef broth
- 1/2 cup sour cream
- 2 tbsp flour
- 2 tbsp butter
- Egg noodles or rice for serving

Instructions:

1. Brown beef in butter, remove, and set aside.
2. Cook mushrooms and onion, stir in flour.
3. Add broth, simmer until thickened, then stir in sour cream and beef.
4. Serve over egg noodles or rice.

Slow-Cooked Beef Chili

Ingredients:

- 2 lbs beef chuck, cubed
- 1 onion, chopped
- 3 cloves garlic, minced
- 1 can diced tomatoes
- 1 can kidney beans
- 2 tbsp chili powder
- 1 tsp cumin
- Salt and pepper to taste

Instructions:

1. Combine all ingredients in a slow cooker.
2. Cook on low for 6-8 hours or until beef is tender.
3. Serve with your favorite chili toppings.

Beef and Guinness Stew

Ingredients:

- 2 lbs beef stew meat, cubed
- 2 cups Guinness beer
- 1 onion, chopped
- 3 carrots, sliced
- 2 potatoes, cubed
- 2 tbsp tomato paste
- 2 cups beef broth
- Salt and pepper to taste

Instructions:

1. Brown beef, then add to a pot with beer, tomato paste, and broth.
2. Add vegetables, simmer for 1.5-2 hours until tender.
3. Season with salt and pepper before serving.

Beef Sliders with Caramelized Onions

Ingredients:

- 1 lb ground beef
- 1 onion, thinly sliced
- 1 tbsp butter
- Slider buns
- Cheese slices (optional)
- Pickles and condiments for serving

Instructions:

1. Form ground beef into small patties.
2. Cook onions in butter until caramelized.
3. Grill or pan-fry patties, melt cheese on top if using.
4. Serve on buns with onions, pickles, and condiments.

Beef Ragu with Pappardelle

Ingredients:

- 2 lbs beef chuck, shredded
- 1 onion, chopped
- 2 cloves garlic, minced
- 1 can diced tomatoes
- 1 cup red wine
- 1 cup beef broth
- Pappardelle pasta for serving
- Parmesan cheese for garnish

Instructions:

1. Sauté onion and garlic, add beef, tomatoes, wine, and broth.
2. Simmer for 2-3 hours until beef is tender.
3. Serve over cooked pappardelle, garnish with Parmesan.

Beef Goulash

Ingredients:

- 2 lbs beef chuck, cubed
- 2 onions, sliced
- 3 tbsp paprika
- 2 cups beef broth
- 1 cup sour cream
- 1 bell pepper, sliced
- Salt and pepper to taste

Instructions:

1. Brown beef, add onions and paprika, cook until onions are soft.
2. Add broth and simmer for 1.5-2 hours.
3. Stir in bell pepper and sour cream, cook for another 10 minutes.
4. Serve with bread or noodles.

Balsamic Glazed Beef Medallions

Ingredients:

- 1 lb beef tenderloin, cut into medallions
- 1/4 cup balsamic vinegar
- 2 tbsp honey
- 1 tbsp olive oil
- Salt and pepper to taste

Instructions:

1. Heat oil in a skillet, season medallions, and sear until browned.
2. Remove beef, deglaze pan with vinegar and honey.
3. Return beef to skillet, cook until glaze thickens.
4. Serve immediately.

Pho Bo (Vietnamese Beef Noodle Soup)

Ingredients:

- 1 lb beef brisket
- 1 lb beef bones
- 2 onions, halved
- 4-inch piece ginger
- 2 cinnamon sticks
- 3 star anise
- 4 cloves
- 1 lb rice noodles
- Thinly sliced beef sirloin
- Fresh herbs, lime, and bean sprouts for serving

Instructions:

1. Roast onions and ginger, then simmer with beef, bones, and spices for 3-4 hours.
2. Strain broth, season with salt and fish sauce.
3. Cook noodles, divide into bowls, add sliced beef and hot broth.
4. Serve with fresh herbs, lime, and bean sprouts.

Beef Carpaccio

Ingredients:

- 1 lb beef tenderloin or sirloin, trimmed and frozen
- 2 tbsp olive oil
- 1 tbsp lemon juice
- Arugula leaves
- Shaved Parmesan cheese
- Capers (optional)
- Salt and pepper

Instructions:

1. Slice frozen beef thinly with a sharp knife.
2. Arrange slices on a platter, drizzle with olive oil and lemon juice.
3. Top with arugula, Parmesan, capers, salt, and pepper.
4. Serve immediately with crusty bread or crackers.

Grilled Beef Satay with Peanut Sauce

Ingredients:

- 1 lb beef sirloin, thinly sliced into strips
- 1/4 cup soy sauce
- 1 tbsp brown sugar
- 1 tbsp lime juice
- 2 cloves garlic, minced
- 1/4 cup peanut butter
- 1 tbsp soy sauce
- 1 tbsp rice vinegar
- 1 tsp sriracha (optional)
- Skewers

Instructions:

1. Combine soy sauce, brown sugar, lime juice, and garlic in a bowl, marinate beef strips for at least 30 minutes.
2. Thread beef onto skewers and grill for 2-3 minutes per side.
3. In a bowl, mix peanut butter, soy sauce, rice vinegar, and sriracha to make the peanut sauce.
4. Serve beef skewers with peanut sauce for dipping.

Beef Empanadas

Ingredients:

- 1 lb ground beef
- 1 onion, chopped
- 1/2 cup green olives, chopped
- 1/4 cup raisins
- 1 tbsp cumin
- 1/2 tsp paprika
- 1 package empanada dough
- 1 egg, beaten

Instructions:

1. Brown beef and sauté onions, then stir in olives, raisins, cumin, and paprika.
2. Roll out dough and cut into circles.
3. Spoon beef mixture onto dough, fold, and seal edges.
4. Brush with beaten egg, bake at 375°F (190°C) for 20-25 minutes, until golden.

Beef Picadillo

Ingredients:

- 1 lb ground beef
- 1 onion, chopped
- 2 cloves garlic, minced
- 1/4 cup green olives, chopped
- 1/4 cup raisins
- 1/2 tsp cumin
- 1/4 cup tomato paste
- 1/2 cup beef broth
- Salt and pepper to taste

Instructions:

1. Brown ground beef with onions and garlic in a skillet.
2. Stir in olives, raisins, cumin, tomato paste, and beef broth.
3. Simmer for 20 minutes, season with salt and pepper.
4. Serve over rice or as a filling for tacos or empanadas.

Beef Rouladen (German Stuffed Beef Rolls)

Ingredients:

- 4 thinly sliced beef sirloin or flank steak
- 4 slices bacon
- 1/4 cup mustard
- 1 onion, sliced
- 1/4 cup pickles, sliced
- 1 cup beef broth
- 2 tbsp flour
- Salt and pepper

Instructions:

1. Spread mustard on beef slices, top with bacon, onion, and pickles.
2. Roll up the beef and secure with toothpicks.
3. Brown the rolls in a skillet, then add broth and simmer for 1.5-2 hours.
4. Remove the rolls, thicken the sauce with flour, and serve.

Beef Sushi Rolls

Ingredients:

- 1 lb beef tenderloin, thinly sliced
- 1 avocado, sliced
- 1 cucumber, sliced into strips
- 1/4 cup soy sauce
- 1 tbsp rice vinegar
- 2 sheets nori (seaweed)
- 1 cup sushi rice, cooked and seasoned

Instructions:

1. Spread a thin layer of sushi rice on a nori sheet.
2. Layer beef slices, avocado, and cucumber on top.
3. Roll tightly and slice into bite-sized pieces.
4. Drizzle with soy sauce and serve with wasabi.

Beef Pho with Fresh Herbs

Ingredients:

- 1 lb beef brisket
- 1 onion, halved
- 1 ginger, sliced
- 4 cups beef broth
- 2 cinnamon sticks
- 3 star anise
- 1 lb rice noodles
- Fresh herbs (cilantro, basil), lime wedges, and bean sprouts for garnish

Instructions:

1. Roast the onion and ginger, then add them to a pot with brisket, broth, cinnamon, and star anise.
2. Simmer for 2-3 hours, then strain the broth.
3. Cook rice noodles, divide them into bowls.
4. Pour hot broth over noodles and garnish with fresh herbs, lime, and bean sprouts.

Slow-Cooked Beef Barbacoa

Ingredients:

- 2 lbs beef chuck, cut into chunks
- 1 onion, chopped
- 3 cloves garlic, minced
- 2 tbsp chili powder
- 1 tbsp cumin
- 2 cups beef broth
- 1/4 cup lime juice
- Salt and pepper to taste

Instructions:

1. Combine beef, onion, garlic, chili powder, cumin, and beef broth in a slow cooker.
2. Cook on low for 8-10 hours until beef is tender.
3. Shred the beef with a fork and stir in lime juice.
4. Serve with tortillas, rice, or as a filling for tacos.

Beef Tostadas with Avocado Salsa

Ingredients:

- 1 lb ground beef
- 1 onion, chopped
- 1 tbsp taco seasoning
- 8 tostada shells
- 1 avocado, chopped
- 1 tomato, chopped
- 1/4 cup red onion, chopped
- Lime juice
- Fresh cilantro

Instructions:

1. Brown ground beef with onion and taco seasoning.
2. Spoon beef mixture onto tostada shells.
3. Combine avocado, tomato, red onion, lime juice, and cilantro for the salsa.
4. Top each tostada with salsa and serve.

Beef Korma

Ingredients:

- 1 lb beef stew meat, cubed
- 1 onion, chopped
- 2 cloves garlic, minced
- 1-inch ginger, minced
- 1/4 cup yogurt
- 1/4 cup cream
- 2 tbsp ground almonds
- 2 tbsp ghee or vegetable oil
- 1 tsp ground coriander
- 1 tsp ground cumin
- 1 tsp turmeric
- 1/2 tsp garam masala
- 1 cinnamon stick
- Salt to taste
- Fresh cilantro for garnish

Instructions:

1. Heat ghee in a large pan and sauté the onions, garlic, and ginger until soft.
2. Add beef and brown on all sides.
3. Stir in the spices (coriander, cumin, turmeric, garam masala) and cook for 2 minutes.
4. Add yogurt, cream, almonds, and cinnamon stick. Stir and simmer for 45-60 minutes until beef is tender.
5. Garnish with fresh cilantro and serve with rice or naan.

Beef and Eggplant Stir-Fry

Ingredients:

- 1 lb ground beef
- 1 large eggplant, cubed
- 2 cloves garlic, minced
- 1-inch ginger, minced
- 2 tbsp soy sauce
- 1 tbsp oyster sauce
- 1 tbsp rice vinegar
- 1 tbsp sesame oil
- 1 tsp chili flakes (optional)
- 2 tbsp vegetable oil
- Green onions for garnish

Instructions:

1. Heat vegetable oil in a pan and cook the eggplant until soft, then set aside.
2. In the same pan, cook ground beef until browned.
3. Add garlic and ginger, and sauté for 1 minute.
4. Stir in soy sauce, oyster sauce, rice vinegar, sesame oil, and chili flakes. Cook for 3-4 minutes.
5. Add cooked eggplant and toss everything together. Garnish with green onions and serve with steamed rice.

Beef Kebab with Moroccan Spices

Ingredients:

- 1 lb beef sirloin, cut into cubes
- 2 tbsp olive oil
- 2 cloves garlic, minced
- 1 tsp ground cumin
- 1 tsp ground coriander
- 1/2 tsp cinnamon
- 1/4 tsp ground cloves
- 1/4 tsp paprika
- Salt and pepper to taste
- Fresh parsley for garnish

Instructions:

1. In a bowl, combine olive oil, garlic, cumin, coriander, cinnamon, cloves, paprika, salt, and pepper.
2. Add the beef cubes and marinate for 30 minutes to 1 hour.
3. Thread the beef onto skewers and grill for 4-6 minutes per side or until desired doneness.
4. Garnish with fresh parsley and serve with couscous or flatbread.

Beef Fajitas with Bell Peppers

Ingredients:

- 1 lb beef flank steak, thinly sliced
- 1 onion, sliced
- 2 bell peppers, sliced
- 2 cloves garlic, minced
- 1 tbsp lime juice
- 1 tbsp soy sauce
- 1 tbsp olive oil
- 1 tsp chili powder
- 1/2 tsp cumin
- Salt and pepper to taste
- Flour tortillas

Instructions:

1. Marinate the beef with lime juice, soy sauce, olive oil, chili powder, cumin, salt, and pepper for at least 30 minutes.
2. Heat a pan over medium-high heat and cook the beef for 4-5 minutes until browned, then set aside.
3. In the same pan, sauté the onion, bell peppers, and garlic until tender.
4. Add the beef back into the pan and stir to combine. Warm the tortillas and serve with the beef mixture.

Steak Diane

Ingredients:

- 1 lb beef tenderloin, cut into steaks
- 2 tbsp butter
- 2 tbsp olive oil
- 1/4 cup brandy
- 1/4 cup beef broth
- 2 tbsp Dijon mustard
- 1 tbsp Worcestershire sauce
- 1 tbsp chopped fresh parsley
- Salt and pepper to taste

Instructions:

1. Season the steaks with salt and pepper.
2. Heat butter and olive oil in a skillet over medium-high heat, then sear the steaks for 3-4 minutes per side.
3. Remove steaks and set aside. Add brandy to the skillet, scraping the browned bits from the pan.
4. Stir in beef broth, mustard, and Worcestershire sauce, and cook for 2-3 minutes until the sauce thickens.
5. Return steaks to the pan and cook for 2 more minutes. Garnish with parsley and serve.

Beef Tamales

Ingredients:

- 1 lb beef chuck, shredded
- 2 tbsp vegetable oil
- 1 onion, chopped
- 2 cloves garlic, minced
- 2 cups beef broth
- 1 tbsp chili powder
- 1 tsp cumin
- 2 cups masa harina
- 1 tsp baking powder
- 1/2 tsp salt
- 1/2 cup vegetable oil (for dough)
- Corn husks, soaked in warm water

Instructions:

1. Heat vegetable oil in a pan and sauté the onion and garlic until softened.
2. Add shredded beef, beef broth, chili powder, cumin, and salt. Simmer for 30 minutes until the mixture thickens.
3. In a separate bowl, combine masa harina, baking powder, salt, and vegetable oil. Gradually add water until a dough forms.
4. Spread masa dough onto soaked corn husks, add beef filling, and fold the husks to seal.
5. Steam the tamales for 1-1.5 hours until the masa is cooked and firm.

www.ingramcontent.com/pod-product-compliance
Lightning Source LLC
LaVergne TN
LVHW081343060526
838201LV00055B/2824